WELCOME TO THE STEAM BATHS. WELCOME HOME.

WRITTEN AND PERFORMED BY **NICK CASSENBAUM** \ DIRECTOR **DANNY BRAVERMAN** \ DESIGNER **BETHANY WELLS**

www.nickcassenbaum.com

Nick Cassenbaum

BUBBLE SCHMEISIS

A storytelling show.
All the stories are true and are performed by the writer.

OBERON BOOKS
LONDON

WWW.OBERONBOOKS.COM

First published in 2019 by Oberon Books Ltd
521 Caledonian Road, London N7 9RH
Tel: +44 (0) 20 7607 3637 / Fax: +44 (0) 20 7607 3629
e-mail: info@oberonbooks.com
www.oberonbooks.com

PB ISBN: 9781786829948
E ISBN: 9781786829955

Cover design: Rebecca Pitt
Internal artwork: Bethany Wells

Printed and bound in the UK.
eBook conversion in India.

Visit www.oberonbooks.com to read more about all our books and to buy them. You
will also find features, author interviews and news of any author events, and you can
sign up for e-newsletters and be the first to hear about our new releases.

Printed on FSC accredited paper

10 9 8 7 6 5 4 3 2 1

Dedicated to
Linda Baylin
Lewis Cassen
Alma Cassen

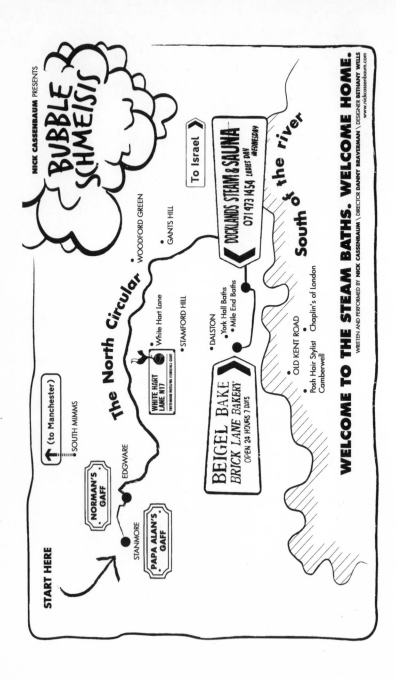

So you bought the book, or you've picked it up and are having a read. What a treat. I couldn't be happier for you.

Firstly if you are just looking in a shop. Buy it? Why not? What harm can it do?

If you have bought it, well done you.

If you are reading a friend's...sharing is caring, but why not get your own version? Then you can write in it, circle your favourite bits...you know have fun with it.

I hope you enjoy it, and if you don't like it. Do me a favour... Keep Schtum.

Original Creative Team
Written and performed by **Nick Cassenbaum**
Director **Danny Braverman**

Assistant Director **Joe Fleming**
Designer **Bethany Wells**
Musicians **Daniel Gouly** and **Josh Middleton**
Other musicians **Tim Karp, Tom Baker** and **John MacNaughton**

Producers have been
Zoe Weldon, Robin Rayner
And for the longest time Sian Baxter

Bubble Schmeisis is a very personal piece. It was a long process of getting it ready to go and I have had a huge amount of support from friends, family, colleagues and organisations

My family
Mandy Cassen (Who sold more tickets than anyone)
Phil Cassen
Abigail Cassen
Alan Greenberg (Papa Alan)
Andrew Green

The men down the baths
Wayne
Eddie
Norman
Tony the One and Only who made my first Bazen
Malcolm

And the rest...

Old Vic new voices.
Simon Longman
Dominic Hodges
Olly Hawes
Matthew Evans

Josh Azouz

Liat Rosenthal

Luke Wallis

Mary Osborn

Emily Harwood

Sean Matthews

Big Wheel Theatre Company

Rogery Hartley

Isolde Godfrey

Barnaby Gibbons

RichMix

Asylum Arts

Louise Mothersole

Rebecca Fuller

Jen Smethurst

Anna Lowenstien

Camden People's Theatre

Robert Ubsdell

Philip Kleinfeld

Howard Gooding

And all the people who financially supported the show at the beginning...

Claire and Michael Martel

Karen and David Saunders

Mandy Cassen

Alison Wilcox

Tracey Levy

Dennis Baylin

Joe Rizzo-Naudi

James Kleinfeld

Richard Grew

Monty

Michelle and Gary Lucas

Andrew Klein

Micheal Symons

Kate Sarley

Gil McDermot

Beverly Collins

Karen Gouly

Abigail Cassen

Zoe Weldon

Caitlin Pearson

Seda Yildiz

Nancy Perrin

Eva Burke

Ezra Schloss

Alex Smith

Graham Brent

Phil and Lorraine Spencer

Erica Greene

Simon Greenberg

Benson Greenberg

Kate Middleton

Sean Meadows

Craig Goldman

Alan Greenberg

Donna Bermange

Elisa and Craig Faugh

Bod de Bois

Alannah Pirrit

John Mapley

Joshua Greene

Dave and Allison Burak

Rob Stoffel

Chris Stoffel

Mel Davidson

Chris Scott

<u>Where the show has been so far…</u>

RichMix
Saturday 5th September 2015
Draft without musicians

Jamboree
Wednesday 16th September 2015, 7pm-11pm
Sections of the show in collaboration with klezmer band Don Kipper.

Camden People›s Theatre
Tuesday 13th October to Thursday 15th October 2015, 7.30pm
First draft with musicans.

JW3
Wednesday 30th March 2016

Camden People›s Theatre
Tuesday 7th June to Saturday 11th June 2016

Summerhall, Edinburgh Fringe Festival
3rd to 28th August 2016

Colchester Arts Centre
Wednesday 19th October 2016

Stratford Circus
Wednesday 16th to Friday 18th November 2016

The Lowry, Salford
Thursday 20th April 2017

Battersea Arts Centre, London
Friday 21st and Saturday 22nd April 2017

The Hub, Leeds
Sunday 7th May 2017

Lawrence Batley Theatre, Huddersfield
Monday 8th May 2017

The North Wall, Oxford
Thursday 18th May 2017

Bike Shed Theatre Exeter
Tuesday 23rd to Saturday 27th May 2017

Wolsey Theatre, Ipswich as part of Pulse Festival
Monday June 5th 2017

Theatre Deli Sheffield
Tuesday June 13th

Macready Theatre, Rugby as part of Festival on the Close
Monday 26th June 2017

Lakeside Theatre, Colchester
Thursday 12th October 2017

Cast Theatre, Doncaster
Thursday 26th October 2017

Bedales Theatre, Petersfield
Wednesday 1st November 2017

Norwich Arts Centre Norwich
Wednesday 8th November2017

artsdepot, North Finchley
Thursday 16th November 2017

Redbridge JCC, Ilford
Thursday 30th November 2017

Aberystwyth Arts Centre, Aberystwyth
Wednesday 6th December 2017

UMS, The Schvitz, Detroit
23rd to 25th March 2018

Seven Arts Space, Leeds
Sunday 3rd June 2018

Soho Theatre, London
Monday 4th to Wednesday 6th June 2018

Blitz, Valletta
Monday 9th and Tuesday 10th July 2018

Manchester Jewish Museum
Thursday 8th November 2018

Neuadd Dyfi, Aberdyfi, Wales
Friday 26th April 2019

The Magnificant Spiegeltent, Nottingham
Wednesday 8th May 2019

The Stepping Stones Pub, Dorking
Friday 4th October 2019

Bowes & Gilmonby Parish Hall, Barnard Castle
Thursday 17th October 2019

Appleby HUB, Cumbria
Friday 18th October 2019

Felton Village Hall, Northumberland
Saturday 19th October 2019

Levens Village Institute, Cumbria
Sunday 20th October 2019

Addlestone Community Centre, Addlestone
Sunday 10th November 2019

Bubble Schmeisis:
the development of a dramaturgical framework for dialogue across difference.

> For theatre to just bring ... comfort, consolation and escape ... that's legitimate. For the next step, ... for its capacity to expose, ... to take the lid off and bring to light the mechanisms, that of course is legitimate. When the two come together, ... can we stop there? ... Or, is there still another level? Is there not a necessity to uncover something more? Which is the human possibilities, ... which in their very nature are positive. [...] Can something be exposed for a brief moment that can bring life to that further dimension: what's it all about? (Peter Brook)[1]

Publishing the text of *Bubble Schmeisis* is an unusual endeavour. After all, this is not a conventional play, it's a piece of autobiographical storytelling only ever performed by its author. Perhaps it will at some point be used as a conventional play text; performed by others, used for scene studies or prepared for auditions. Nevertheless, my guess is that this script will principally be used as a record of a process; a process that is still ongoing, because as I'm writing this, Nick and his musical collaborators are still touring to venues in the UK and beyond.

At its essence, storytelling is *re-telling* and every show is a new iteration, a unique moment of co-creation with the audience as an essential co-conspirator. As the play's director, and by some definitions its dramaturg, I hope this introduction to *Bubble Schmeisis* will give you a flavour of our dramaturgical

---

[1] Brook, P. (2010). *'Meetings with Directors': Lecture given by Peter Brook with Richard Eyre | Digital Theatre*. [online] Digitaltheatreplus.com.

journey. Most of all, I want to describe how we developed a new framework to bring together all the elements that we think make a good show. Note, I use the term *show*, not *play* or *performance* or *production*. I like the word *show*. It bundles our endeavour with other kinds of popular performance; with pantomimes, comedy and music gigs. It starts with the assumption that our audience is going to have a good time, that we're on their side, no matter what their background. Most of all, a *show* is class-inclusive; you won't be made to feel that you don't 'fit in', as you might with some other theatre.

Hopefully, this introduction gives you a tool to examine Nick's script; a particular written record of words, actions and music. With conventional plays, the script is a series of instructions for the collaborating artists. It assumes the primacy of the writer, providing a similar function to a composed score in classical music. Performers, scenographers, musicians, directors and so on are *interpreters* of authorial intent. But, the process of creating *Bubble Schmeisis* was not this conventional one. This introduction, then, will outline another way of 'doing dramaturgy' – working on the rehearsal room floor, trying things out in front of audiences, continuously reflecting and evaluating, then developing the show again for the next version. Indeed, *Bubble Schmeisis* is still being re-created in every performance. Perhaps here, we can see that the word *production* is the least adequate to describe our show. Thankfully, it will never be that stale thing, a finished product, it is always process.

As with all culture, *Bubble Schmeisis* exists in a socio-political context. Since the first scratch performance in 2015, the world has changed and so the show's meaning constantly shifts as well. I would argue that even though the content of much theatre addresses pressing contemporary issues, it is still not adequately responding to a dynamic socio-political landscape. Communities around the world are fractured, with nationalism and tribalism of all kinds on the rise. Meanwhile, our theatre is driven by a market-led approach, mesmerised by the notion of the "target audience". In fact, cultural experience as a whole is almost entirely characterised by forms of exclusivity. Sporting events, for example, are highly gendered (mostly male); religious gatherings are definitively exclusive; and live music is clustered by genres that attract audiences, to a large extent, on the basis of their gender, race, class and age. It prompts the question of where we can find a more inclusive live experience and what kind of form a performance should take that makes a virtue of attracting people from all backgrounds. To that end, just as Nick took his own story into rehearsals, I took an idea for a new dramaturgical framework. That framework, Dialogue Across Difference (D-a-D), aims to find ways of making theatre that is hopeful, democratic and, above all, inclusive. It is worth saying here, that D-a-D, like *Bubble Schmeisis* itself, will never be complete. The dramaturgical framework is also always process.

The idea of D-a-D first occurred to me when trying to work out why my own solo show *Wot? No Fish!!* 'worked'. I put 'worked' in quotation marks here, as it's a term used ubiquitously amongst theatre-makers and is notoriously woolly. I stumbled into *Wot? No Fish!!*. I found the family treasure of my Great-uncle Ab's wage packets, with weekly drawings of family life stretching across fifty-five years. Collaborating with director Nick Philippou, we made a show out of this extraordinary find and, following a successful Edinburgh Fringe run, found that bookers, reviewers and, most of all, audiences gave it an overwhelmingly positive response. Audiences reacted in a number of ways. When I was performing, there were palpable responses. Not just laughter, but utterances, sighs, murmurs of recognition and so on. This show seemed to 'work'. Taking into account audience 'vox pops', I noticed four distinct kinds of reaction. Firstly, there was a sense of communality in the audience, regardless of differing backgrounds. Particularly, it was noticeable that the show brought people together across generations and cultural boundaries. Secondly, people were weeping and simultaneously expressing gratitude, indicating a sense of catharsis/release, deeply personal experiences were being felt. Thirdly, some of the laughter and other audible utterances were clearly generated by the ideas in the piece; light-bulb moments of realisation. Lastly, there was a sense of uplift and joy – somehow the experience had been profound and memorable.

Whilst trying to fathom, then, how and why *Wot? No Fish!!* 'worked', I found myself, obliquely, talking to my Goldsmiths' colleague Gerald Lidstone about marketing. He pointed me to the work of marketing consultancy Morris Hargreaves MacIntyre (MHM) and their identification of four key drivers for cultural engagement: the social, the intellectual, the emotional and the spiritual (Morris Hargreaves MacIntyre, 2007)[2]. This clearly chimed with the combination of factors that had 'worked' with *Wot? No Fish!!* What the MHM model does not do is connect these audience drivers to theatre-making methodologies.

So, when Nick Cassenbaum approached me to direct his solo *'schvitz'* piece, it was an ideal vehicle for a practice-as-research project to develop a D-a-D framework. Our research methodology used a "'hermeneutic-interpretive' spiral model, where progress is not linear but circular; a spiral which constantly returns us to our original point of entry but with renewed understanding" (Trimmingham, 2002)[3]. In this case, it was not just the show that was subject to this paradigm, but also the D-a-D model itself; constantly reviewed and adjusted

[2] Morris Hargreaves MacIntyre (2007). *Audience knowledge digest: Why people visit museums and galleries, and what can be done to attract them.* [online] Manchester. Available at: https://webarchive.nationalarchives.gov.uk/20120215211331/http://research.mla.gov.uk/evidence/documents/Audience%20Knowledge%20Digest.pdf [Accessed 28 Jun. 2019].

[3] Trimmingham, M. (2002). A Methodology for Practice as Research. *Studies in Theatre and Performance*, 22(1), pp.54-60.

in the light of the practice. Our investigation, then, was to explore how the four MHM strands – the social, intellectual, emotional and spiritual – could inform the show's dramaturgy, specifically to create a bridge across difference for audiences.

Bubble Schmeisis went through a number of iterations, each informed through a series of 'scratch' performances. It grew as much through reflecting on audience response, as it did on the rehearsal room floor. It became increasingly clear that the most effective shows enabled audiences to simultaneously hold an individuated and a communal experience. This is best summed up by the idea of an *audient*, an individual audience member that becomes a proxy for us all. Early on, in role as Norman (the lump of *lockshen*), Nick interrogates an audient, to demonstrate Norman's particular brand of cantankerousness. Nick improvises dependent on the audient's response. "Where did you get your shoes from?" He'll often ask. Of course, responses are many and varied and the exchange is playful. Other audience members will inevitably be enacting simultaneous internal dialogues with the belligerent Norman, partly relieved and partly envious of the audient in the temporary limelight. How would they manage being put on the spot so confrontationally? This simple exchange sets a tone for the rest of the show. The story invites us to draw connections to the particularity of our own prospective responses to parallel situations, while at the same time – as we will find out as the story progresses – there are universals that unite us. Difference, whether it is about identity or personality, is not division; finding your 'tribe', your sense of belonging (a controlling idea of the show), does not mean we don't share a common humanity.

Social-bonding through attending performances comes naturally to us, but is often derailed when we feel we don't fit in. Nevertheless, as MHM demonstrate, a key motivator for attending performance is to share it with someone; to strengthen our bonds to them. Maybe we buy two or more tickets and then consider who to invite. The choice of a partner, friend or relative signifies a common journey we want to take with them. Maybe we feel a need to strengthen a bond and choose the performance as a way of starting out on a journey of shared meaning. Once we get to the site of performance, we then encounter people we don't know and the signifiers at the venue. Naturally, that's when we ask ourselves whether we fit in. Every aspect of the experience up to the beginning of the performance, from the journey to the venue to the ushering in to the performance space, is loaded with signification. Many of these signifiers affect the experience and so are a critical component of a show's dramaturgy. With a touring show like *Bubble Schmeisis*, a lot of meaning is contingent on the venue. Foyer displays, front-of-house welcome and bar prices (if there is a bar and it is open) are all loaded with meaning. If theatre is to break out of niches and create a welcome that transcends differences, then it is vital to create an atmosphere that doesn't unwittingly exclude.

So, beginnings are vital for creating the social bonds in an audience that bring about what the anthropologist Victor Turner termed *communitas*[4]; a sense of temporary community. This is a challenge for the average studio theatre. Very often, through their architecture and design, these are unwelcoming spaces, despite the best intentions of programmers. With *Bubble Schmeisis*, Nick uses his street theatre skills to start the process of building *communitas* in the foyer. As they come in, audiences are greeted by the duo's klezmer music and by Nick, all three wear bathrobes and flip-flops and Nick gently chats to people to welcome them. The costumes clashes with traditional foyer expectations and the music has that peculiar Jewish mix of minor melancholic notes and dance rhythms. Nick chats warmly, like the host of a party, making each audient feel welcome. They are aware, of course, from Nick's attire that they are in the presence of a *performer*. The tone is set, we feel

[4] Turner, V. and Schechner, R. (1995). *The anthropology of performance*. New York, N.Y.: PAJ Publications.

at home. Subliminally, the theme of feeling 'at home', of being welcome and comfortable, has been introduced. Whatever your background, the tone of playfulness and warmth is set. We the audience are guests, and we're led across the threshold to the auditorium.

As if by magic, the performers are now in the playing area. Nick is busying himself with setting things up – again the host, putting out food and preparing tables, although not with tablecloths so much as beach towels. Other furnishings obviously belong to the theatre – their generic plastic seats. Nick has a metal-mesh locker on wheels. You can glimpse some fruit, a faux-silver platter and a large orange bucket. The signifiers here are that this will be a bit of rough theatre, we're not expected to marvel at fancy sets and lighting. The musicians are now playing Lionel Bart's *Consider Yourself*, the klezmer version. Nick breaks into the audience, has a good look at the various objects and checks everything's in place. He's constantly acknowledging us, smiling, saying hello.

Casually, Nick now greets us for the first time as one entity. He's chatty, introduces himself and the band and sparks our imaginations by setting up the various rooms of the Canning Town *Shvitz* with brief spoken descriptions of the various rooms of the steam baths; words triggering images. All the time, Nick checks in with the audience, bouncing rhythms back and forth, acknowledging contributions, no matter how unusual, and deftly folding them into the event with a sense of playfulness. The convention that the band will punctuate the proceedings with musical stings is set up. Nick refers to the room he never goes in: ' ... that's for the Russians, not for me,' he says – the band plays a few bars of a clichéd Russian theme. We get the joke; we laugh together. As he would in the steam bath, Nick then breaths in and out and encourages us to breath with him. This is a form of call-and-response as found in different forms in many performance rituals: the stand-up getting a cheer from hen and stag dos; the evangelical preacher corralling 'amens'; the West African griot storyteller's drumming and chants. Our audience journey so far has enabled us to discard our individual everyday anxieties, prejudices and assumptions. Our imaginations have been engaged to co-create, belief has been built in this peculiar version of a *schvitz*. We feel assured and comforted in the capable hands of a relaxed storyteller; but, we also know to be alert. This is a performer that will break the fourth wall. You never know, I – or perhaps the person sitting next to me – may be called on to take part. However, we know from Nick's demeanour, that this will be achieved with kindness. This will not be a performance where any audient is humiliated.

Thus, the social bonding that *Bubble Schmeisis* gently encourages, particularly with those we *didn't* choose to come with, is fundamentally a political act of bridging difference. The warmth of Nick's performance style and the avoidance of any 'author's message' throughout avoids agitprop. Although, as we will see, we will share his discomfort later when hotter issues are addressed.

As Nick and I sat around kitchen tables and jumped about in rehearsal rooms, we made structure a central concern of the developing dramaturgy; a structure rooted in taking our audience on a satisfying emotional journey. As with many first drafts of plays, *Bubble Schmeisis* was initially a pick-and-mix of treats, but it needed concerted thinking about sequence and foregrounding to enable our audience to travel with Nick on his journey. It quickly became clear that our metaphorical journey would be an actual one, along the A406 North Circular Road, and the quest myth (see Propp[5] and Campbell[6]) was the obvious scaffolding. We then derived great enjoyment plotting our version of the Tribes of Israel in the light of London-Jewish experience and giving each tribe its location along the legendary A406.

[5] Propp, V., Wagner, L. and Scott, L. (1969). *Morphology of the folk tale*. Austin, Tex.: University of Texas Press.

[6] Campbell, J. (2008). *The hero with a thousand faces*. Novato, Calif.: New World Library.

Although this structure had the built-in risk of becoming too episodic, and thus perhaps distancing our audience in a way that was too Brechtian for our purposes, we felt that keeping a strong sense of Nick's super-objective, to find his cultural 'home', would carry the audience with us. At this point it became clear, that to structure an effective emotional journey, we needed to think naturalistically, even though the piece as a whole is stylised. Accordingly, we borrowed eclectically from the Stanislavskian toolkit[7]. However, we made a differentiation between two modes of performance. Storyteller-Nick, as opposed to character-Nick, would focus on his super-objective, to ensure that the audience would have an over-arching emotional experience. Character-Nick would materialise through deft role-shifts, each moment having a specific intention under the umbrella of storyteller-Nick's super-objective. So storyteller-Nick embarks on his quest to find identity and meaning through the lens of character-Nick slaying the dragons of ardent young Zionists, Spurs fans and antisemitic South London barbers.

Although these incidences are culturally very specific, as the saying goes: 'you don't have to be Jewish'. The creation of Nick's stage persona, an amalgamation of the storyteller and the role-shift personae, was critical for the audience to drive round the North Circular in his shoes. In a sense, the Nick Cassenbaum in *Bubble Schmeisis* comes in a long tradition of the 'innocent abroad'; he is naïve and optimistic, so we know from our experience of other narratives that he is likely to prevail. Literally a child in some of the episodes, there's a universality in Nick's childlike bewilderment and instinctive emotional responses to the strange, new lands he encounters. Each of us has had an analogous experience of encountering unfamiliar environments and asking ourselves what they mean for the formation of identity.

[7] Stanislavsky, K. and Hapgood, E. (2015). *An actor prepares.* [United States]: Aristophanes Press.

Bubble Schmeisis layers its raw emotional moments with humour, but this is a humour grounded in self-deprecation, so there is a sense of reassurance being in the hands of storyteller-Nick, while at the same time we feel the discomfort and frustration of character-Nick. Perhaps this admixture of warmth and unease is best epitomised by the moment when character-Nick finally has to reveal his naked body in front of his Papa Alan and his cronies, having delayed the moment for some time:

> We are back in the *schvitz* ... and it is time for my *schmeiss*. And of course I have to get naked.
> *Open wrap ... reveal boxer shorts ...*
> What do you expect for (*insert ticket price*) pounds?
> As I walk into the *schmeiss* room Norman says to me, 'you don't have to wait for your grandad if you want to come again, come on your own.' And Eddie says the nicest thing he has ever said to me and the nicest thing he will ever say, 'yeah and don't worry boy. We all have tiny cocks.'

Of course, the playing of the *'reveals boxer shorts'* moment is critical to engaging audience feeling. In the section above, character-Nick doesn't speak – but the *action* is the role-shifted character-Nick. For storyteller-Nick, it is vital that he triggers our imaginations. He invites us to build our own pictures of these old hands at the *schvitz* through character-Nick's eyes. We all know, not just the males in the audience, that this exposure could lead to terrible humiliation. So, the long pause (represented by an ellipsis in the script) builds a tangible tension. The relief in performance, when Norman and Eddie speak their approval, is the tangible exhalation of laughter. It is relief for us all. We are going through it with character-Nick. Thus, the social experience is deepened by an emotional, communal experience, brought about by the oscillation between storyteller- and character-Nick.

As the D-a-D model developed further, we acknowledged that the majority of popular performance is light on substance. In some quarters, there's an assumption that too much overt intellectual content can put off audiences. On the other hand, MHM have demonstrated that audiences actively seek out intellectual stimulation from culture. We are, after all, by nature a curious species; one that wants to increase our knowledge and understanding of the world. What we don't want, is to be told what to think or made to feel excluded because we don't have the cultural capital so often implicit in 'high culture'.[8] The challenge with *Bubble Schmeisis* was to find ways that the themes and ideas in the show could provide an inclusive intellectual experience. So, we based our approach on critical pedagogy; a dialogic approach that doesn't set up the artist as an authority, but akin to Augusto Boal's 'joker'[9], a figure that creates a forum for fresh ideas to flourish. We were not interested primarily in fact-based knowledge acquisition, but in inviting our audience to develop conceptual thinking; tools for reflecting on their own place in the wider world. In this way, the narrative spiral keeps returning to the familiar motifs of Jewish identity; the tribe, the Promised Land, diaspora experience and disputation. However, these are clearly universal themes. Given that we aimed to embrace equitably the diversity of audience experience, there could not be one 'correct answer'; the story functioned as a tool for each audient to reflect on their own experiences. There are infinite dialogues here: internal; between audients; between an audient and the show's characters; and between each audient and those not present at the event. Some of these dialogues may actually take place, but many of them will be private. They are ways for us to understand a bit more about the world and our place in it. Each audient will bring their own experience

[8]   Bourdieu, P., Passeron, J., Nice, R. and Bottomore, T. (2014). *Reproduction in education, society, and culture*. Los Angeles: Sage.

[9]   Boal, A. (1979). *The theatre of the oppressed*. London: Pluto Press.

to bear and it is impossible for any artist to know what that is. Our role then, is to provide a platform for as rich a learning experience as we can.

The moment when Nick experiences the Western Wall during his trip to Jerusalem was one of the most powerful moments in performance. Nick has a disturbing response to the prayer wall – he cries, and yet there's a sense that he's been manipulated. The monstrous Stacey Pinkus informs Nick that 'this is your tribe'. And yet, in her attempts to cement solidarity to spiritual Zionism, Stacey has not converted the secular Christopher. When Stacey invites the gathering to suggest a song, Christopher chirpily proposes *Consider Yourself*. The resonances in this short section are manifold, opening up provocations from a number of perspectives, but all contingent on the particular experience and knowledge-base of an audient. The idea of tribal belonging is once more foregrounded. For a religious Zionist, of course, this could be uncomfortable: where does a secular Jew fit in with their world view? Perhaps for another audient this moment brings to mind the original context of the song; written by Lionel Bart – a gay, secular Jew. For others, Jews and non-Jews, the universal themes go deeper than the specifics of Jewish identity. When Christopher is denounced by Stacey, disparaging him by the use of the term 'yok', it is a shockingly aggressive act. The universal questions here are about exclusion from a 'tribe'; not just for Christopher or Nick, but also for each individual and, perhaps more crucially, for those that we may, perhaps unwittingly exclude ourselves. So, on the surface the audience are pulled in to the narrative and react, typically, with alarm and then the release of laughter. However, at the same time *Bubble Schmeisis* is confronting a central question for the age of Trump, Brexit and the rise of toxic nationalism: how can we have both a strong sense of identity and at the same time be generous and inclusive?

Perhaps the biggest challenge to developing Dialogue Across Difference has been how to identify and talk about a spiritual experience. After all, spirituality is a slippery term by definition; it cannot be measured or authenticated. Having said that, in discussions in rehearsal, Nick and I were eager to pin down what it meant in terms of making a show. One of the challenges for performance is that we live in a world awash with the products of the cultural industries, leading to the commodification and disposability of art of all kinds. Our daily routine is punctuated by playlists, podcasts, advertisements and Netflix. We asked ourselves: what differentiates the best of performance experience that can make it contribute significant meaning to our lives? That can rise above the everyday? It soon became obvious, that a key element to the spiritual dimension of performance is that the impact is long-lasting and *memorable*. We discussed shows that had given us an elevated experience, moments where we felt *uplifted*. So, both in rehearsal and during performance runs, we tried out different ways of telling our story with the aim of making it *memorable* and *uplifting*.

Just as the social dimension has its foundations in beginnings, so the spiritual is about endings; a satisfying culmination to the experience. There are two endings in *Bubble Schmeisis*: the *schmeiss* itself, when an audient ritually washes Nick on stage, and Nick's final *beigel* rant. The *schmeiss* is the culmination of character-Nick's journey. An audient, the proxy for us all, is now in the role of Papa Alan and there is an act of cleansing; spiritual and actual. We are complicit in this initiation ceremony; we are all accepted into this tribe. Our sense of *communitas* has led to this moment; it is joyous, side-splittingly funny and somehow very moving. In performance, the exhilaration of the *schmeiss* is almost always accompanied by loud cheering, laughter and applause. The *beigel* rant is storyteller-Nick's final moment, confirming his sense of identity. Nick stands on the table as the rant gets increasingly fanciful:

And then the tikka-touts, the ones that sell curry down brick lane, they run up, and they join in shouting, "beigel, beigel, beigel." Then a herd of Hipsters run round from Shoreditch high street station, and they join in shouting, "beigel, beigel, beigel." (Band start playing *Consider Yourself*, quietly at first, then getting louder') Then, then I have a look, and I can see Barbara Windsor, and the Mitchell brothers and Dot Cotton, and they join in shouting, "beigel, beigel, beigel." Then an old black roller pulls up down the end, and out come the Kray Twins, and their old mum, and they start going, "beigel, beigel". Then I see a chorus line of chimney sweeps, girls selling matchboxes, women selling oranges, costermongers, and a plethora of pearly kings and queens, and they're all going "beigel, beigel, beigel, beigel... beigel..."

Nick has drawn a picture of a specific location, the Brick Lane Beigel Bakery. He has taken us all there. Despite the rant being about cultural specificity, it is also an inclusive vision. Jews are an integral part of the very English idea of an East-End London identity, as are the curry house families, the cockneys and the hipsters. The rant is a parody of a rousing political speech, with all the rhetorical flourishes and passion that are expected. In performance, as often as not, audiences of all kinds would join in with the *beigel* chant – an act of solidarity.

A constant rehearsal question was to identify the elements contributing to the spiritual dimension. My feeling now is that there is no absolute recipe, but contributory factors are a sense of catharsis (albeit not of the strictly Aristotelian kind), intellectual light-bulb moments when we feel a sense of a mystery being revealed, moments that have symbolic, ritual resonance and a strong sense of sharing an uplifting experience as a unified audience. More analysis of how the social, emotional and educational elements of a performance experience bring this about is needed, but in *Bubble Schmeisis*, the D-a-D model, judging from audience reaction, seemed to 'work'.

Danny Braverman
Theatre-maker and Lecturer in Theatre & Performance, Goldsmiths
June 2019

A NOTE ON THE MUSIC.

When putting together the music for Bubble Schmeisis, we were determined to draw the repertoire from very traditional sources. Since the show is very much about getting in touch with roots and tradition in a modern world, we wanted to reflect this in the music. While there are many musical jokes in the show, like the nokia ring tone etc, the music itself is very much from traditional klezmer repertoire.

The only piece of music in the show which is not traditional klezmer (aside from the sound effects!) is 'Consider Yourself' though it would be wrong to say that we don't 'klezmerise' it a bit. The choice of this tune is a) the message in relation to Nick at home in the schvitz, and b) a nod to a Jewish composer.

When choosing the repertoire, we made decisions based on several factors.

The first is simply theatrical, for example the tune for the first part of the journey round the north circular *Hongu and Freylekhs'* is a tune with lots of forward momentum and helps build the pace of the action onstage.

The second is more meaty, and is for comic juxtaposition or to make a reference, comic or otherwise. For example the piece for South Mimms service station is a *Doina,* which is a traditional Klezmer lament. This adds a melodramatic edge to what is otherwise a very banal location. It also links the goodbye between mother and son to the possibly final farewell at the kindertransport in WW2. The vast and therefore comic gap between these two realities (the Berlin railway station in 1938 and the Hertforshire service station in 1996) is the kind of thing that only music could link.

Another example of a reference is the tune which is played for Nick's experience in South London. The tune in question is *Der Terk in America* by Naftule Brandwein the self-proclaimed 'king of the klezmer clarinet' (and not many would argue with this). One's yiddish doesn't need to be top-notch to get the gist of the meaning, and so we decided to take this story of a pilgrim in a foreign land (the Turk in America) and position Nick as the wanderer in the foreign and strange land of South London, the place where 'no Jew has been before'.

Posh the hairstylist marches Nick down the Old Kent Road to *Firn Di Mekhutonim Aheym* 'Leading the In Laws Home', again a traditional tune repurposed, and you can find these kind of references dotted throughout the show.

Our aim in keeping to traditional repertoire was really to emphasis this link with the old world, and to give the message of surviving tradition against all odds, both in Jewish music and how we wash each other.

Josh Middleton

Music is often about journeys, as is this show, and Jewish music, and particularly Klezmer has had a turbulent journey through the 20th and 21st centuries. From shtetl obscurity, to the soundtrack of burgeoning European metropolises, to success and translation in the new world, and ultimately to mid-century loss and then revival in modernity across a myriad of Jewish and non-Jewish spaces.

Bubble Schmeisis not only tracks our journeys together performing across the UK, Europe, and America, but those taken by generations of Jews in the diaspora in which traditions, such as those of the schvitz and Klezmer music, help to bind us together as mishpoche.

In the music we choose we try to illuminate these myriad journeys in our lives and the lives of so many others, to bring to life the wonderful stories that make up the show.

Daniel Gouly

BUBBLE SCHMEISIS

On stage is a table and empty chair. There a cage Locker on wheels full of the props for the show. The musicians are sat on chairs playing **Traditional Klezmer Freylekhs**. *As they play NICK sets up the scene, he greets the audience whilst putting three wraps on the table. He goes into the audience and chats to them. When the band start playing 'Consider yourself' NICK stands by the table and waits for them to stop. He is wearing a rope and wrap his grandfather gave him and flip-flops that used to be his Uncle Steve's.*

Hello everyone...hello everyone... *(Wait for audience response.)* Thanks for coming.

My name is Nick, for those of you that don't know me. And this is Josh and this is Dan. Has anyone here been to the schvitz before? Anyone?

React to audience response.

Ok, don't worry.

Because we are now in the schvitz. And the schvitz is a place to relax, so relax, get comfortable on your seats, and together we are all going to breathe. So breathe in, breathe out. **(Accordion player 'breathes with bellows at the same time, and for any breath hereafter throughout the play.)** Fantastic. breathe in, breathe out, breathe in *(wait a prolonged amount of time)...* breathe out... that's it. Very good... don't stop breathing whatever you do.

During this NICK is pointing out the locations of the different areas of the Schvitz.

This is the schvitz. The Canning Town Schvitz. The floor is covered in tiles. The walls are covered in tiles, and the ceiling is covered in tiles. If you look the tiles are white and green with dirt wedged between the grouting. Over there are a line of sinks, and here is a line of shower heads, because you've

got to have a shower before you have a schmeiss. And over here is the first of the wet steam rooms. That's where you schmiess. And there's another one there and there, and they go down in temperature. That is the hottest one. That is the one I use. Over there are the dry steam rooms, the saunas, but that's not for me. That's for the Russians.

(Play first 4 bars of 'Katyusha' Russian Folk Tune.)

We are surrounded by white garden furniture and a marble bench. In case you get too hot, behind you is a plunge pool. Upstairs there's the cafe where you can get a bite to eat, and sofas where you can sit down and watch the football. Back down here if you come a lot, you get your own locker. *(NICK taps the locker.)* And whilst we recline we eat fruit *(NICK gets out each piece of fruit from the locker and places them on top of the locker)...* banana, melon, oranges and pineapple. You know... fruit.

This is the Canning Town schvitz, a place to get your mind cleansed and your bum-hole cleaned.

Breath.

So you may be thinking why a young man of *(Enter how old... at the time of this edit...31)* is here in a schvitz, a place usually reserved for *alta kakas...* old men.

Well I'll tell you; I speak to my Papa Alan about three times a week on the telephone. He would like to have it more but

20

I try to limit it. And my Papa Alan is short, round and his mince pies are going, that means he's going blind. But he has a talent. No matter what road you are on in London, he can tell you what's on that road, what's around that road, and how to get from that road to any other road in London. If it wasn't for his minces he'd probably be a cab driver. And he grew up in Dalston in East London when it was a very Jewish area, and when we are on the phone that's what we talk about. We talk about the salt beef gaffs that are gone, the beigel shops that aren't there anymore, the markets, and the Jewish businesses, but he never seems to know where the synagogues were. But one place he talks about with real reverence one special place is... the schvitz. But as he explains, most of them are shit now. Ironmonger row, that's shit now. Mile End baths, that's shit now. York Hall, that's shit now. But there is one proper schvitz left in East London, and that is here. The Canning Town Schvitz.

And one day I'm on the phone to him *(SFX phone ringing from accordion, **Nokia Theme Tune** on on accordion piccolo reed.)* *(NICK gets up and picks up the banana and uses it as a phone)* and he goes:

"I am going to the schvitz tomorrow".

And I said, "You're not".

And He said, "I am".

And I thought this is it. This is my chance to go to the schvitz for the first time ever with my Papa Alan. So I said, "Well I am coming with you then" and there was silence on the other end of the phone.

Then I said, "Hello", and he said, "Hello".

I said, "I am coming with you".

He said, "No you're fucking not".

I said, "I am".

He said, "Fuck me". I said, "I won't do that, but I will come with you". He said, "Okay, come over to mine, stay the night and in the morning we will go".

So, *(places the banana on the pineapple to look like a phone)* I made my way over to the promised land... **(band play first phrase of 'Hatikvah')** Stanmore, and I stayed the night. In the morning he hands me this robe and this wrap, and we wait to be picked up. And then we hear a honk from outside. **('Honk sound effect on accordion, two notes 1 tone apart, single coupler.)** I schlap my Papa Alan to the end of the drive and there is this pristine white Mercedes. And sitting behind the wheel with both hands on it and spiked up hair is, the famous Eddie Bloom, who gives the best schmeisis in London. I open the door and schlap Papa Alan in the front, and I jump in the back, Eddie says, "Watch the carpet; just had it cleaned", and we're off. But before we leave the land of milk and honey of North West London we have another pick up to make. Now Eddie hardly says a word the entire drive, but one thing he does say is "We have to pick up the lump of lockshen".

Now does anyone here know what lockshen is? *(Ask the audience.)* It's the noodles you have in your chicken soup and you can make a pudding out of it... it's like vermicelli only more globby. And I like it; I like it in a soup and like it in a pudding but, I had never heard anyone described as a lump of lockshen before. So I was curious.

We pull up outside a bungalow in Edgware with an old black cab on the drive.

Eddie, once again he honks the horn. And I look out the window and then the front door slowly opens... and as it opens... it reveals *(As NICK puts his arm up SFX of **Chromatic**

scale from bottom to top of accordion keyboard.) the tallest
Jew I have ever seen in my life. Could have been seven foot.
And as he walks towards the car **(clarinet plays low broken
chords, dotted crotchet – quaver, dotted crotchet – quaver)**
with his long arms, his long legs, and his pot belly, the only
words I can use to describe him are… a lump of lockshen. He
opens the door and there is Norman. And as he looks down at
me he says, "Who the fuck is this?"' and my Papa Alan goes,
"That's my grandson, that's my boy." Then he gets in the car
seat next to me and he starts asking me questions; question
after question after question after question…

Go up to a member of the audience and start asking them questions;

What's your name?

What do you do for work?

Make a lot of money?

How'd you get here today?

Where did you get your hair cut?

Where did you get your shoes from? *(Improvise this as
appropriate.)*

Thank you very much round of applause for…

So Norman was asking me all these questions and as *(insert
audience member's name)* can probably tell you, it felt like an
interrogation.

But after a while I had to block out these questions, because
what suddenly came to mind was that within the hour, these
three men were going to see me completely naked. And my
Papa Alan had never seen me naked. My Papa Alan had
never seen… my schmakel. But I thought actually it was going
to be ok… because what with his minces he wasn't going to

23

see a thing, especially not my schmakel. But what about the other two men? Well, you know there was going to be a lot of steam down there so that might cover me up… But what about all the other men down there? They were all going to see me naked for a prolonged period of time. But then I thought actually it was going to be ok…because you know we've all been through the same thing… You know, when you are 8 days old, you put on a massive spread, you invite the whole family round, and you watch a baby have half his schmakel cut off. So at least we all have the same schmakels.

   Breath.

But there was a time **(musicians play 'Hora with Onions underscoring)** when I thought my schmakel was different to other schmakels. I'm at primary school and I'm seven years old, and at my primary school we had one of those long tin silver urinals. You know what I am talking about? The silver urinals? Like troughs? And at the bottom of the urinals we had those little orange cakes that are there to **(accordion plays high A minor Arpeggio)** freshen up the gaff. And I'm there and I am taking a pish. *(Standing as is at a urinal using the robe cord to look like penis, adjusting the size of it.)* And as I am pishing, I see the cake move a bit. **(Accordion low trill.)** *(Running along the stage as is moving the cake.)* So I pish the cake up, **(accordion Glissando up keyboard)** and I pish the cake down. **(Accordion Glissando down keyboard.)** I pish the cake up… **(Accordion Glissando up keyboard.)** I pish the cake down. **(Accordion Glissando down keyboard.)** As I am about to go for the third rotation I hear the door go. **(Clarinet plays decending major 3rd interval.)** I turn. I look, I see ginger hair and freckles… it's Dudley Gabriel. Boy in my class. And Dudley comes and plonks himself right here **(clarinet plays single note)**… He doesn't know the code. Even at seven years old I knew the code. That when you are having a pish you always leave a gap between you and the person next to you. But Dudley Gabriel, bold as brass, comes and plonks himself right **here (clarinet plays single note)**. So we're both there pishing standing next to each other.

And you know I'm seven years old... I am curious... I've been to Spain, but other than that I have barely been out of Woodford Green. So I decide to have a little look... see what Dudley's got. So contort myself round and have a look *(Bend down to look. SFX clarinet squeak.)* Sorry... But there's something going on here...there is something different going on here... So I go in for a closer look. *(Bend right down.)* By this point I'm finished so I'm just holding my schmakel staring at his.

Dudley finishes, washes his hands, and I do the same. I go back to class and all I can think about is Dudley Gabriel's schmakel. Dudley's got something extra on the end. It looks like he's got a piece of bacon wrapped round the end of it. I'm in the car on the way home and all I can think about is Dudley Gabriel's schmakel. I get in the house and all I can think about is Dudley Gabriel's schmakel, and so I say to my mum, "Mum, Mum what's wrong with me?'... and she says "What do you want a list?".

"No, with my schmakel. What makes my schmakel so different from all other schmakels?' She says, "Ah you'll thank me when you're older... it's cleaner, and girls prefer it" and apparently I signed a contract before I could hold a pen.

Breath.

Band play 'Hongu' from 'Hongu and Freylekhs from Podoly'.

We're back in the car. And now we've hit the North Circular. And the North Circ is a very important road to these men, It's the road that separates these men: from the land they live in now, and the land where they grew up. From the land that they live in now, to the land they couldn't wait to get away from. From the land that they live in now, to the land that they

25

schlap back to twice a week to have a wash. As soon as we hit the North Circ **(band change to 'Freylekhs' from 'Hongu and Freylekhs from Podoly')** we go past a turning now if you go up this turning you eventually get to Potters Bar and the M25 but on this turning is a very famous service station. and it's called *(Band Stops suddenly.)* ... South Mimms. **(Band play loud dramatic Doina, which drops in volume after first phrase for underscoring.)** And South Mimms is an important service station because once a year it gets chock-a-block with Jewish parents dropping off their kids to go on Summer camps. **(Doina rises in volume for one phrase then drops down again.)** And I am no exception to this. I'm fourteen years old. My mum she drops me off... she grabs me by the jacket. She kisses me on the cheek. **(Clarinet plays high 'kvetch' klezmer technique for the kiss.)** She says, "Nick... Nicky... Nicholas... have a lovely time, enjoy yourself. But do yourself a favour... **(doina stop)** get your end away".

I get on the coach and I see a sea of children from North West London and they are singing this song ...We are FZY... **(Clarinet player joins.)** We are FZY... **(Accordion Player joins.)** WE ARE FZY...that's the Federation of Zionist Youth. I find myself a seat next to someone who is not singing. I see glasses, white trainers, and head in a handkerchief. I think he is hiding from the singing, but no, he is hiding a nosebleed. It's Eric Goldfarb.

We pull up to where the camp is going to be. We are all put in a great big hall and we wait to meet our leader. I sit over here with Eric and all the other Jews from Essex. And then... she walks into the room.

> *NICK becomes Stacey Pinkus* **(Stacy Pinkus theme: Low accordion drones in clashing intervals, clarinet plays clashing low notes.)**

Her arms go out to reveal 10 *chipollatas* hanging off the end of her *lappers*. Her tightly wound black hair is blowing in the cheap air conditioning. And her mouth opens to reveal the shiniest set of braces I have ever seen in my life, with a piece of spinach sticking out of it. Probably from her morning frittata. She says, **(music stops)** "My name is Stacey Pinkus and I will be your leader for the next two weeks. They will be the best two weeks of your life. Look around you; you have met your tribe… *(NICK asks for the lights to be put up so the audience can see each other – their 'tribe', then house lights down again.)* But before you go off and enjoy yourself, let's see who we've got here shall we? *(NICK makes each section of the audience and gets them to wave.)* Over here we have the people from Hampstead… the intellectuals everyone. Hi there! This side of the room, it's the religious ones… it's the people from Hendon. Hello Hendon. And this side of the room, it's my home crowd, so I know they are going to be noisy. It is the Golders Green and Temple Fortune massive. Hiya!… You did not disappoint. And she's come all the way from Manchester, and she's sat all the way at the back there… But she's my cousin, so Hampstead boys, hands off. It's Linda Pinkus… Hi Lind. And of course we have… the Essex Jews. So everyone enjoy yourself and I will see you all later. Yalla."

Later that night i'm sat in my room with my roommate, Eric Goldfarb, and I am contemplating my escape, when I hear a knock at the door. **(Accordion player 'knocks' on accordion.)** I say to Eric… "Get the door" **(accordion knock)** … he says "You get the door"… **(accordion knock)** I say, "You get the door"… **(accordion knock)** he says, "You get the door"… **(accordion knock)** I say, "You get the door"… **(accordion knock)** he says, "You get the door" **(accordion knock)** I say, "Ok, ok, I'm coming". I go over to the door, and as I turn the handle a little bit the door is kicked in and I'm thrown back. I look, and there is a figure all dressed in black, with a balaclava on, holding what looks like a… what looks like, a

machine gun *(grabs the banana)*. Shouting, "Out Jew scum".
I turn to Eric and he is quivering under his duvet, and I think
to myself, "I should have gone to Marbella". I look a bit
closer, and I see that the machine gun is made out of plastic,
and surrounding it are five chipolatas. **(Musicians play 'stacy
pinkus theme'.)** I look closer and hanging out of the balaclava
is tightly wound black hair, and shining in the moonlight, it's
those braces. There at my door with a plastic machine gun
shouting, "Out Jew scum" is… **(Music stops.)** Stacey Pinkus.
She frog marches me and Eric into the hall where we first
met. We sit with all the other Jews from Essex.

She takes centre stage. She says, "You have all been taken
hostage… you were on an aeroplane heading to Israel and
we have brought you here to Entebbe airport in Uganda, and
you will remain here until all our demands have been met.
(Mimes pulling up balaclava.) Out of role. In the 1970s a plane
full of Jews heading for Israel was taken over by Palestinian
terrorists, and they were taken to Entebbe airport in Uganda
the IDF saved them. But one brave soldier lost his life… his
name Yonatan Netanyahu."

I turn to Eric Goldfarb, I say. 'Netanyahu… that doesn't
sound like a Jewish name'.

Eric is hyperventilating **(clarinet breathing)** … he says
"where's my inhaler?" **(Stop clarinet breathing.)** Stacey
Pinkus pulls back **(musicians play Stacy Pinkus theme)** on
the balaclava, comes up to us and says, "And you… you're
the worst of all… Essex Jews"

 Breath.

We're back in the car, and we're stuck in traffic for the turn off
for the M25. My Papa Alan turns to Eddie and says, "Eddie
you schmok we shouldn't have come this way. We wouldn't
be stuck in traffic if we had gone another way". Eddie's hands
tighten around the steering wheel, but he says nothing. And

as we sit in traffic I look at the turn off, and it reminds me, as if I hadn't learnt my lesson, one year later I was back at South Mimms; this time to go on a month long trip to Israel. My mum grabs my jacket, kisses me on the cheek, and says, "Have a lovely time and this time, do yourself a favour, get your end away", and then she slips a condom into my pocket.

I get onto the coach…once again the children from North West London are singing, "We are FZY… **(Clarinet player joins.)** We are FZY… **(Accordion Player joins.)** WE ARE FZY… his time Eric Goldfarb has learnt the words, he's singing along, and he's waving his inhaler in the air.

I find a seat next to someone who isn't singing. I see a pair of espadrilles, powder blue shorts and a Ralph Lauren shirt. I sit myself down. I say, "Hello", he says, "Hello"… I say, "What's your name?" He says, "My name's Christopher". I said, "Nice to meet you, I'm Nick. What are you doing on this trip?" He says, "My grandmother is a Jewish person… she's about to die and she wants me to see Israel before she goes". I said, "Lovely… my mum just wants me to get laid, but looking round I don't think that's going to happen". I offer him the condom. He takes it and says, "She only gave you one… for a month?" "She's realistic".

We're on the aeroplane now and before I know it we're flying over Israel… and I see someone I recognise coming down the gangway… *(NICK becomes Stacey Pinkus.)* The arms go out to reveal the chipolatas, the tightly wound black curls are waving in the air conditioning, and the mouth opens… and the braces are gone… and let me tell you, the teeth look fantastic. She says, "My name is Stacey Pinkus, and I am like Moses leading you to the promised land. Look out the window and you will see it you will see the land that was once nothing. We took that land and built a something. We turned that dream into a reality". We land… We all get on a coach and we're schlapped out into the middle of the desert. Stacey Pinkus picks up a handful of sand. She says, "See this sand.

See this sand. This sand used to cover the entire country. We took this sand and we built a country. We turned this dream into a reality". We get on the coach and we are taken into the centre of Tel Aviv. Stacey takes us into a shopping centre and she stands under the air-conditioning. **(Clarinet player stands up, points clarinet at Nick and breathes down it, making air noise.)** "Feel that air-conditioning, feel it. We brought air-conditioning here, before us there was no air-conditioning, we turned this dream into a reality". **(Stop Clarinet Breathing, clarinettist return to seat.)** We go outside and go past a cafe where some people are eating. Stacey picks up a pot of hummus from their table. "See this humus, see this humus. We brought humus here, before us there was no humus. We turned this dream into a reality".

It's our last day, we get onto the coach and she goes, "shhhhhh", she says "we are going to go to the place where it all began, the place there the dream was dreamt that became a reality, we are going to… **Yerushalaim' (Accordion plays static drone, clarinet plays doina from 'Doina and nachspiel by Naftule Branwein as underscoring.)** We drive into the old city in complete silence and are taken off the coach one by one and we walk toward the western wall. and I see a sea of men in black coats and black hats and they're davening, they're praying. Just as I'm about to walk towards the wall, Stacey puts her hand on my shoulder and she says, "This is it Nick, these are your people. This is your tribe". And I walk towards the wall. I manage to weave my way to the front, but I don't know what to do, so I put one hand on the wall like this, and the other like this. And I stand staring at the wall. As I am staring I can hear a noise next to me. It sounds like a crying…a weeping. **(Clarinet player makes sobbing sounds with clarinet using 'krechts' klezmer technique.)** I turn and I look, it's Eric Goldfarb. And he's crying and weeping and he can't stop. I turn back and look at the wall . I can feel something coming down my cheek. And I realise that I'm crying, and weeping and I can't stop.

After a while we're all ushered away from the wall (**clarinet stops, accordion drone continues**) and we stand in a circle holding hands. I look round at the group and I see everyone has been crying... but there is one person who isn't crying... it's Stacey Pinkus. She says, "I knew this would happen, you have all now dreamt the dream that has become a reality... Let's sing a song. Any suggestions?" (**Accordion drone stops, musicians look at the ground.**) I look around and everyone else is looking at the ground. But there is one person who hasn't been crying; I see the espadrilles, the powder blue shorts and the Ralph Lauren shirt and it's Christopher... and he says, "I've got a song we can sing, let's sing "Consider Yourself"... you know, *(NICK sings)* Consider yourself at home, consider yourself part of the family, come on Stacey"... Now Stacey Pinkus is staring at him, giving him complete evils. And she says a word. The rudest possible word for a non jew... She says... "YOK".

Breath. (Band play 'Oytseres' as underscorring.)

We're back in the car. And we're out of the traffic by the turning for the M25 and driving along the North Circular. We are about the go past a turning for Tottenham. Now if you go down that turning you eventually get to White Hart Lane where Tottenham Hotspur play. Now, from the day I was born I was destined to be a Tottenham Hotspur fan… and when I reached six it was going to be my first game. I'm in my room wearing my brand new kit I got from JD Sports in Enfield the weekend before, and I am excited. And then I hear my Dad shout from downstairs, "Nick come on we are leaving now." My Mum says, "What are going now for? The game doesn't start for an hour and it only takes 20 mins to get there." My dad says, "I am not getting stuck in traffic. We're leaving now." **(Music stops.)** In the car, Five Live on the radio and we are off.

We park up in a school playground they rent out for a car park on match days. I open the door and see a hopscotch, 1-2-3 I've done it and we are off, walking towards the stadium. As we get closer I see a man selling scarves, I say, "Dad, Dad, can I have a scarf?"… He says, "No they're crap"… I say, "OK they're crap"… when we get closer to the stadium I see a man selling hot dogs, I say, "Dad, Dad, can we get a hot dog?" "No they're crap"… I say, "OK they are crap". Then we get to stadium, and I see it in front of us… and I see a police horse do a massive shit on the floor. We go up into the stadium and there's a man selling programmes, I say "Dad can I have a programme?" He says, "No they're crap", I say "OK they're crap."

We walk out to the stadium and I see the green pitch in front of me. I turn and I see a sea of empty blue plastic chairs. I look at the clock… we're 40 minutes early. We take our seats. As we wait other people start to arrive **(accordion plays rhythmic pattern basses, clarinet plays 'When the Saints**

Go Marching in') … Friends, families and fans start arriving and crowd out the seats. Then they start cheering and the atmosphere is growing. Then all the players come on. Then the ref comes on, puts down the ball and blows his whistle. **Accordion plays high cluster chord on piccolo reed for 'whistle sound effect', previous music stops.)** From behind me there is a collective… groan. **(Band play decending glissando, and drop into slow and unsteady blues as underscorring.)**

He kicks the ball to him… to him… to him… and I'm bored. I look at the clock… 5 minutes… to him… to him… him… 6 minutes. I look around for something to entertain me. I see that the symbol is a chicken sitting on a beach ball… that's quite good. 6 and half minutes. To him… to him…I'm starting to fall asleep, feel my eyes going… think I mustn't, I am here with my Dad… but just as I'm about to nod off I hear this noise.

(Band joins on 'Booms'with instruments and on 'YIDS' with voices.) BOOM BOOM BOOM BOOM YIDS… What's that? And it goes again, BOOM BOOM BOOM BOOM YIDS . I say, "Dad Dad", he goes, "What?" I said, "Dad what's a Yid?" He goes, "What?" "A Yid?" He goes, "A Yid… a Yid… a Tottenham fan. Me, I'm a Yid. You, you're a Yid. Everyone over here, Yids. Them, Yids. Opposite us, Yids. On the pitch, look, Yid Yid Yid… he's a Yid, always will be, Sol Campbell. Ones down there, they're Yids. But up the ones up there in the black and white, with their tops off singing, they ain't Yids. They're Geordies". I think oh… I'm a Yid!

Half time comes, I want a snack, not allowed one, they're crap too. Second half, score's nil-nil, 20 mins in Dad wants to go, doesn't want to get stuck in traffic. Back in the car, Five Live on the radio, 92nd minute Spurs score, winning 1-0. Dad says, "Fuck, I missed it. Sounds crap anyway." We get in the house. Mum says, "Did you enjoy yourself?" Dad goes, "No it was crap". "Nick did you have a nice time?" I shake my head, and I think to myself, why do these men do it? Why do they go to this place to be miserable? They don't buy scarves, they don't buy hot dogs, programmes or snacks, and they're not even happy when they win. So I say to my mum, "I don't think I want to be a Yid"… She says, "Nothing would make me happier than telling your dad that. You're not going to meet a nice girl there anyway."

Breath. **(Band play 'Dem Monastrishter Rebin's Chosidl' as underscoring.)**

We're back in the car. We go past the turning for Tottenham. Now if we had gone down that turning we would have gone through Stamford Hill which is where the Frummers live, the Stamford hillbillies who are either in shul, going to shul, or coming out of shul, something to do with shul. We would have cut through Clapton and come to Newham that way, but instead we keep going round the North Circ. Papa Alan says, "Eddie you schmok we should have gone that way it would have been quicker." Eddie says, "Shut up Alan." **(Band suddenly stop.)** And he does. **(Band suddenly start again.)** We keep going around the North Circ. We go past Woodford, where I grew up. We go past Ilford and Gants Hill, which is where my dad is from, and then we come up into East London. And as soon as we hit East London the atmosphere in the car suddenly changes. *(Band change from playing 'Dem Monastrishter Rebin's Chosidl' in a bulgar rhythm to the same song in a 'terkisher' rhythm, and continue.)*

… Eddie starts talking, Norman stops asking me questions and it's almost as if Papa Alan's minces start working, as they recognise every street corner. "That's where that one had a business that went kaput". "That's where that one and that one had an argument and they still ain't talking". "That's where that one and that one met and they are still schtupping". And I'm desperately trying to see these places. But I gotta tell you it looks completely different to me as it does to them. And then we arrive in an industrial estate in Canning Town. **(Band stop and play Doina version of 'ConsiderYourself' as underscoring.)** I look out of the window. I see a blue sign and in white writing it says: The New Docklands Steam Baths… The Canning Town Schvitz. **(Music stops.)**

I schlap my Papa Alan out of the car, and slam the door. Eddie says, "Watch the paint work".

The first place we hit it the locker room. As soon as we hit the locker room I realise not only were they going to see me naked… but I was going to see them naked. And I have never seen my Papa Alan naked. I turn to my locker and I prepare myself for… the vision. I turn and I look. I see that the three of them have got their robes and their wraps on, and they are ready to go.

My Papa Alan shouts… "Nicky are you ready come on?" Norman says, "He ain't ready, why ain't he ready? What's wrong with him?" I say, "I'll meet you down there". They go, and I make sure the coast is clear, and I put on this robe, and this wrap, and I make my way down to the schvitz. From the bottom of the stairs I hear my Papa call, "Nicky this way" as he goes down.

When I get to the top of the stairs I start to hear the showers hitting the floor. **(Accordion makes tapping sound on bellows.)** As I get closer, I can hear the men, and they're rucking at each other. **(Clarinet makes 'arguing sounds'.)** And as I get closer I can make out what they are saying, some are rucking about Spurs, some are rucking about a do one was invited to and one wasn't, some are laughing, and some are singing songs and schticking themselves. **(Musician sound FX get louder.)** And then I get down there and I see a sea of pink, hairy, wrinkly, sweaty flesh. I realise that it's gone completely schtum. **(Music stops.)** And all eyes are on me… And then I hear a voice from the corner of the room shout,

"Who the fuck is that?'" And Papa Alan grabs my arm and says, "That's my grandson, that's my boy"

And I notice one big difference between me and them... they've all got their robes off... so I take mine off too.

NICK takes the robe off.

And from that moment on I'm blind Alan's boy. Everyone wants to know me. Everyone wants to talk to me, everyone's trying to suss me out, everyone wants me to sit next to them. But Papa Alan drags me to sit with him and the other pilgrims from our journey. And as I sit there they open their wraps to reveal themselves. And there they are, in all their glory.

Each piece of fruit represents one of the men. As NICK says each name he gets a piece and puts it onto the wraps on the table. Eddie is a pineapple, Papa Alan a melon and Norman the banana.

The famous Eddie Bloom, with the spiked-up hair, who looks remarkably good for a 75 year old man. My Papa Alan, who wasn't going to see my schmakel because of his minces, I wasn't going to see his because of his great big belly. And Norman, the lump of lockshen, who has a piece of lockshen, and two kneidlach. *NICK makes a hand gensture signaling picking up two small balls.* And me... *(Make out NICK is going to open his wrap.)* I crossed my legs. I wasn't ready to reveal myself.

Breath. (Band play 'Der Terk in America' as underscoring.)

As I sit there reflecting on my journey, a journey that ended where the North Circular hits the River Thames, it reminded me that there is another world out there. A world where no London Jew should go, where no London Jew is now, and where no London Jew will go again... and it's called **(music stops)** South of the river. But I went there. And not only did I go there... I lived there. **(Accordion plays 'wrong answer' sound effect.)** And when I lived there I needed my hair cut, believe it or not.

And one day I'm walking down Deptford high street and I see this lovely-looking old barber shop called Chaplin's. And I went in, and it was lovely. Lovely leather barber seats, lovely clean floor without a hair on it, lovely big mirrors, those cylinders of blue liquid, and most importantly; a cut-throat razor. I never go into a barbers unless they have cut-throat razors, means they do a proper job.

So I went in and I said, "Can you fit me in?" The geezer said, "Did you book?" I look round and the place is completely empty. "No, but can you fit me in?" He says, "Certainly sir, take a seat."

So I sit down and he gets the clippers out and starts shaving my head.

NICK stands behind the chair shaving a head with the banana.

He's shaving away and he says, "Isn't London changing?" I say, "Yeah, it's changing". Then he goes, "Have you seen them buildings out outside?" I said, "No". He said, "Have a look? See em?" I said "Yes." "Have another look, see em?" "Yes". He says, "Do you know who owns all them buildings?" I go, "No." He goes, "Do you know who owns all those buildings?" I go, "No." He goes, "Do know who owns all those buildings?" I say, "No." He says, "They own all them buildings, sir, but you'll never see them come round here, sir. They never come round here, sir."

I said, "Who are you talking about?"

He says, "They never come round here, sir, cos they are scared to come round here, sir."

I said, "Who are you talking about?" He goes, "They own all those buildings, sir, but you'll never see them come round here, sir, cos they are scared to come round here, sir"

I said, "Who are you talking **about**?" *(Pause.)*

"They own all those buildings, sir, but you'll never see them come round here, sir, cos they are scared to come round here, sir"

He goes, "The Jews. They own it all. They own all those buildings, sir, but you'll never see them come round here, sir, cos they are scared to come round here, sir."

So I said, "That's funny."

NICK puts down the banana walks and sits in the chair.

He goes, "Why's that funny?" I go, "That's funny." He goes, "Why's that so funny?"

I say, "Cos I'm one of them."

Then he went completely schtum, and he put down the clippers… And he picked up, the cut-throat razor *(Picks out a leaf from the top of the pineapple.)* Completely schtum, and he takes it and he just starts to shave round the back of my head. *(NICK demonstrates with the leaf.)* Completely schtum and he takes my ear like that and he just shaves, completely schtum, then he takes it and just goes round the bottom of my neck here. *(Using the tray the fruit was on uses it as a mirror to show the back of the head.)*

I go, "Lovely". And I give him a generous tip and I leave.

Breath.

We're back in the schvitz, and I see men going into the schmiess room white, and coming out pink like a cooked lobster. Every so often a sweaty head would come out the plastic curtains and say something like, "Will someone come and finish Manny off?" And go back in. You see the schmiess is the main ritual of the schvitz, he *piece de resistance.* And with any ritual there are commandments. And as I sit with the three men they bestow the commandments upon me.

#1. **(Clarinet klezmer-style fanfare.) Always** wear flip flops. You do not want to spread verrucas. *(**Musicians indicate their flipflops.**)*

#2. **(Clarinet klezmer-style fanfare.)** If you are going to sit with your bare arse out, put down a wrap. You don't want your touchas being where anyone else's has been.

#3. **(Clarinet klezmer-style fanfare.)** We all schmeiss each other. We all work. Do not be a schmeiss ponce.

#4. **(Clarinet klezmer-style fanfare.)** Never complain about the heat of the schmeiss, that's probably the most broken rule of the schvitz.

#5. **(Clarinet klezmer-style fanfare.)** You wait your turn.

#6. **(Clarinet klezmer-style fanfare.)** When you are having a schmeiss you have to be naked.

And it was almost my turn, so of course I had to get... naked.

Make out about the get naked, but don't.

But before that.

(Band play 'Der Terk in America' as underscoring.)

I realised I was about to be inaugurated into my tribe of men. And It reminded me of a time when I was on my own. I was tribe-less in the wilderness of South London. When I was at my loneliest. It's 3 o'clock in the morning, and I'm drunk walking down the Old Kent Road, when this man came up to me and stuck his hand out to me like that *(stick out arm with a flat palm (in an audience member's face)* **(band do short chord sound effect)** right in my face. Right in my face. Just like that **(band do short chord sound effect)** *(stick out arm with a flat palm in an audience member's face)*, I'll do it one more time over here like that, *(stick out arm with a flat palm in an audience member's face). **(Band do short chord sound effect.)** And I didn't know what to do, I'd never been accosted in such a way before. So I did the one thing I felt I should do. The only thing I could do. I grabbed it like that. *(Clasp hands together.)*

And the man went, "Oh my god."

I said, "What?"

He said, "Oh my god."

I said, "What?"

He said, "You are the first white man to ever grab my hand like that."

I said, "You must be joking."

40

He said, "No."

And then he said, "You must be a Jew or a Muslim or something."

So I said, "Yeah, I'm Jewish."

He said, "Oh my god."

I said, "What now?"

He said, "You're the first Jew I've ever met."

I said, "You're joking."

He said, "No."

And then he put his hand around my shoulder and then he **started to march** me down the Old Kent Road. **(Band Play 'Firn di Mekhutonim Ahem'.)** He said, "This is my Jewish friend. This is my Jewish friend. This is my Jewish friend." And I'm there shaking everyone's hand. "Nice to see you, nice to meet you... nice to have you."

And after I'd met about 80 percent of the population of the Old Kent Road we find ourselves outside this club. **(Music stops.)** And it's packed, and it's pumping out Afrobeats music. Afrobeats music... *(Looking to musicians who refuse to try to play that music.)* Afrobeats, forget... And he says, "You are my guest in here tonight". I looked at the club, it's half three in the morning, and I thought I can't be bothered.

So I said, "I'm tired, it's late, I'm going to bed".

He says, "I like you. You are serious man."

So I say to him, "What's your name?"

He goes to me, "I will never tell you my name."

So I say to him, "What's your name?"

He says, "I will never tell you my name."

I said, "What's your name?"

He said, "I will never tell you my name."

I say, "Go on tell us your name."

He goes, "OK. I'll tell you my name." And he rolled up his sleeve, and tattooed on his arm,

was the word posh. And he said, "My name is Posh, cos everyone listens to me."

I said, "Nice to meet you Posh. My name's Nick."

Then he takes out his business card, and he hands it to me, and he says, "We are gonna make a lot of money together."

I looked at the card and it was white with a gold border, and in black letters it says, Posh, hair stylist, Camberwell. I said, "Nice to meet you Posh", and go to walk off. Then he says, "Hold on, I've got a question for you", I said, "Yeah?" He says, "Let me ask you a question." I say, "Go on". He says, "Let me ask you a question." I say, "Go on ask me the question."

He says, "Let me ask you a question."

I said, "Go on"

"What is wrong with you Jews?"

I said, "What?"

He goes, "What is wrong with you Jews, huh?'

I go, "What do you mean?"

42

He goes, "What is wrong with you Jews huh, what you causing so much trouble for?"

I said, "What are you talking about... who are you talking about... what Jews are you talking about? Do you mean the Hampstead Jews, or the ones from Hendon or Golders Green? Do you mean the Essex Jews? Or the chasids down in Stamford Hill? Or do you mean the Yids down at White Hart Lane? Or perhaps you mean the property developers? Or the Northern Jews from Manchester or Leeds? Or do you mean... do you mean David Beckham, he had a Jewish grandparent? Or do you mean Woody Allen? Are you talking about Woody Allen, or do you mean me? You don't mean me, do you Posh?'"

And he says, "You Jews... what you causing so many problems for?"

So I **said**... "I'm sorry... I'm sorry."

Breath.

We are back in the schvitz... and it's time for my schmeiss. So of course I have to get naked.

Open wrap... reveal boxer shorts...

What do you expect for *(insert ticket price)* pounds?

And as I walk into the schmeiss room Norman says to me, "You don't have to wait for your Grandad if you want to come again, you can come on your own." And Eddie says the nicest thing he has ever said to me, and the nicest thing he will ever say to me, "Yeah, and don't worry boy, we all have tiny cocks!"

Ok it is now time for my schmeiss. Boys can we have some schmeiss music please. **(Band play 'Flatbush Waltz' as underscoring.)** Right, so you are going to give me a schmeiss.

(Gets a member of the audience. NICK shows the member how to schmeiss. Giving them what they need. Then NICK lies on the table and the audience member schmeisses him.)

Round of applause please. Now, have you ever given a schmeiss before? Well you are going to be fantastic. Just stand here and I am going to get you everything you need to give a schmeiss. So this is a bazen, this is what you are going to schmeiss me with. Bazen is Yiddish for mop. And this is a bar of soap, also very important for the schmeiss. So what is going to happen is, I am going to lie here, and you are going to get the soap and the bazen and rub me up and down… ok? Great.

So Eddie took my wrap wet it and put it on my head. Then I lay on the table and my Papa Alan started to schmeiss me… GO FOR IT! **(Band play louder.)**

Fantastic… **(Band drop in volume.)**

Then my Papa Alan said the words I never thought he would say as I lay completely naked… he said, roll over. And I did, and then he schmeissed the front. **(Band play louder.)**

(Schmeiss finishes.)

Please give… a big round of applause.

Thank you very much. **(Band play rubato version of 'Behusher Khosid' as underscoring'.)**

Breath.

After the schmiess I found a nice quiet spot to sit on my own. And I felt so nice, so clean. I had just been inaugurated into an age old tradition brought over from Eastern Europe, and I felt part of something. There I was sitting with all these naked, swearing, shouting men, and I didn't give a monkeys any more. I felt at home. More at home than I ever felt going to

Tottenham. More at home than I ever felt going to shul. More at home than I ever felt in Israel... I was at home. **(Music cadences to finish.)**

After the schmeiss it is customary to have something to eat, and I have brought you all some oranges to have after the show. But the oranges didn't quite cut it for me after my schmeiss, so I got the boys to drop me off at the only place worth eating in East London, and that is the beigel shop on Brick Lane. Do people know this place? Yes? Good. If you don't then you have to go there.

And you'll notice how I say beigel... and I am very militant about this. Because the Jews that brought the bread with the hole, or the hole surrounded by bread, to London, they were from Poland, and their way of saying it was beigel. But the German Jews who took it to America, their way of saying it was bagel. So we should say beigel, they can say bagel... they can say beigel if they want.

So I was in the shop and I was gonna order my usual, that's a chopped herring with pickle and a cream cheese with pickle. The pickle is 20p extra... I think it's worth it. And in front of me is a city boy. Got nothing against city boys. And he goes, "Yah, give me one of those salt beef bagels... no mustard"... I mean, what's the point?

I didn't say anything. He took his bagels and left, and I ordered my beigels and then I went outside. When I got outside, I saw this man leaning on the bin, stuffing his face with the salt beef bagel. I thought, "I've got to say something". So I went up to him and I said, "Excuse me."

He said, "Yah."

I said, "That's a beigel"

He said, 'What?'

I said, "That's a beigel, and when you ordered it you said bagel."

He said, "Whatever."

I said, "No, not whatever, it's a beigel."

He said, "I don't care."

I said "No, not I don't care, it's a beigel and we should say beigel, cos if we stop saying beigel then that voice, that specific London Jewish voice will be gone, and dead, and lost forever.

He said, "Leave me alone"

"No, not leave me alone. It's a beigel, it's a beigel, beigel, beigel, beigel, beigel, beigel, beigel. And then, a homeless woman came up to me. She said, "I've lived here my whole life, and its beigel." And then she put her arm around me and the two of are shouting, "Beigel, beigel, beigel, beigel, beigel."

And then, the old Irish lady that works in the shop, she came up and said, "Yeh, I'm sick of people calling them bagels, they're beigels, and then the three of us are shouting, "Beigel, beigel, beigel."

And then the tikka-touts, the ones that sell curry down Brick Lane, they run up, and they join in shouting, "Beigel, beigel, beigel." Then a herd of Hipsters run round from Shoreditch High Street station, and they join in shouting, "Beigel, beigel, beigel." **(Band start playing 'consider yourself', queitly at first, then getting louder'.)** Then, then I have a look, and I can see Barbara Windsor, and the Mitchell brothers and Dot Cotton, and they join in shouting, "Beigel, beigel, beigel." Then an old black roller pulls up down the end, and out come the Kray Twins, and their old Mum, and they start going, "Beigel, beigel". Then I see a chorus line of chimney sweeps, girls selling matchboxes, women selling oranges, costermongers, and a plethora of pearly kings and queens, and they're all going, "Beigel, beigel, beigel, beigel… beigel…" **(Band loose tempo and pitch and end up on drone, they then continue playing consider yourself very slowly and quietly as a Doina, rubato.)**

After a while I realise it's just me… and the homeless woman.

Eventually the man walked off, and I go to do the same, but the woman shouted, "Oi beigel, beigel, I helped you out there, the least you can do is buy me a beigel."

I said, "Where are my manners?"

And I put my hand in my pocket, and I pulled out a two pound coin, and I put it in her hand.

And she said, "Let bagels be beigels."

Then I started to walk away from Brick Lane, eating my beigel. And I thought to myself, "One day, am I going to be the only person who calls it a beigel?"

Then I thought about the schvitz, I mean these are old boys. In 30, 40 years time… who is going to be schmeissing?

Then I thought to myself, and who am I going to give their first schmeiss to? **(Music stops.)**

Let me know if you want it to be you!

(Band play 'Consider Yourself' at tempo.)

END

YIDDISH GLOSSARY

Alta kakas	Old Men
Bar Mitzvah	Rite of passage; becoming a Jewish man
Bazen	Raffia brush used to schmeiss
Beigel	Bread with a hole / hole surrounded by bread
Briss	Circumcision
Broygus	Argument
Bubbemeises	Grandmother's story / tall story
Davening	Praying
Frummers	Hasidic jews
FZY	Federation of Zionist Youth
Gantze macher	Big-timer / big shot
Kneideluch	Dumplings
Kvetch	Complain, moan
Lockshen	Egg noodle
Pish	Piss
Punim	Face
Schlap	To drag
Schmakiel	Willy
Schmeiss	'to hit'; cleaning ritual of the baths
Schmeisser	The person doing the schmeissing
Schmok	Idiot
Schticking	Laughing
Schtum	Quiet
Schtupping	Sex
Schvitz	Sweat
Shul	Synagogue
Simcha	Do / party / celebration
Touchus	Bum
Yid / Yiddo	Tottenham Fan
Yiddishe	Jewish
Yok	Non-Jewish

EAST LONDON GLOSSARY

Punters	People
Minces	Eyes
Gaf	Place
Butchers-hook	Look
Starkers	Naked
Rucking	Getting into a fight
Do	Party
La Di Da	Cigar
Lappers	Hands

WWW.OBERONBOOKS.COM